TABLE OF CONTENTS

ACRONYMS vi

ILLUSTRATIONS viii

TABLES ix

INTRODUCTION 1

THE CLOCKS 4

    The Washington Clock 8
    The Theater Clock 11
    Summary 13

THE VIETNAM WAR FROM 1955 to 1975 15

    The Vietnam War from 1955 to 1964 ~ Limited Partnership 17
    The Vietnam War from 1965 to 1968 ~ Americanization 22
    The Vietnam War from 1969 to 1975 ~ Peace with Honor 29
    Summary 37

CONCLUSION 39

    The Washington Clock Has Not Started ~ OEF-P 40
    The Theater Clock is Ahead of the Washington Clock ~ OEF-Afghanistan (2001-2009) 42
    The Washington Clock Forces the Theater Clock to Speed-Up ~ OIF (2006-2008) 43
    Summary 44

APPENDIX A: MAP 46

BIBLIOGRAPHY 47

ACRONYMS

AFP	Armed Forces Philippines
ANA	Afghanistan National Army
ANP	Afghanistan National Police
ARVN	Army of the Republic of [South] Vietnam
CAS	Saigon Office of the U.S. Central Intelligence Agency
CARL	Combined Arms Research Library
CGSC	U.S. Army Command and General Staff College
CHMAAG	Chief, Military Assistance Advisory Group
CIA	Central Intelligence Agency
CIP	Counterinsurgency Plan
CORDS	Civil Operations and Revolutionary Development Support [pacification]
CTZ	Corps Tactical Zone
DMZ	Demilitarized Zone separating North and South Vietnam
DOD	Department of Defense
DRV	Democratic Republic of [North] Vietnam
FEA	Bureau of Far Eastern Affairs in the State Department
HES	Hamlet Evaluation System
HNC	High National Council
I Corps	Northern military region of South Vietnam
II Corps	Central military region in South Vietnam
III Corps	Military region in South Vietnam surrounding and including Saigon
IV Corps	Mekong Delta
JSOTF-P	Joint Special Operations Task Force - Philippines
LOC	Lines of Communication
LRC	Light Reaction Company
MAAG	Military Assistance Advisory Group

MACV	Military Assistance Command-Vietnam
MMAS	Master of Military Art and Science
MOD	Minister of Defense
NSAM	National Security Action Memorandum
NSSM	National Security Study Memorandum
NSC	National Security Council
NVA	North Vietnamese Army
NVN	North Vietnam
OEF	Operation Enduring Freedom
OEF-P	Operation Enduring Freedom - Philippines
OIF	Operation Iraqi Freedom
OND	Operation New Dawn
PAVN	People's Army of [North] Vietnam
PNG	Provisional National Government
RVN	Republic of [South] Vietnam
RVNAF	Republic of Vietnam Air Force of Armed Forces
RVNF	Republic of Vietnam Forces
SAMS	School of Advanced Military Studies
SVN	South Vietnam
USG	United States Government
VC	Viet Cong
VM	Viet Minh
VN	Vietnam
VNA	Vietnamese National Army

ILLUSTRATIONS

Page

Figure 1. Foucault's Pendulum. 5

Figure 2. Newton's Cradle. 5

Figure 3. The Pendulum Metaphor...6

Figure 4. The inner workings. 10

Figure 5. The Washington clock. 10

Figure 6. Trends in American domestic support and opposition of the Vietnam War...................20

TABLE

Page

Table 1. Popular reasoning for the Vietnam War...21

INTRODUCTION

> The society that separates its scholars from its warriors will have its thinking
> done by cowards and its fighting done by fools.[1]
> — Sir William Francis Butler, British General Officer

More than two hundred years since the American Revolution, the civil and military

discourse continues to shape how the United States employs its military forces and the manner in

which it fights wars. Perhaps the most renowned public official and tactician that acknowledged

this discourse was General George Washington. Washington accepted the fact that "Americans

judged military actions by results…[p]ublic opinion and political leaders were intolerant of

generals who failed to get results."[2] Washington was keenly aware of this demand to

continuously produce results within a short amount of time with minimum cost to lives. He

planned campaigns with not only the public in mind, but the Continental Congress as well.[3] The

pressure to achieve desired outcomes while competing against a clock set by civil authority

constrained how Washington practiced operational art. This issue became extremely important for

American generals like Washington to act not only decisively, but also to constantly give the

appearance of action. As a tribute to Washington's military genius in understanding this friction

in war, an iconic artifact is an ongoing display at the Metropolitan Museum of Art. This artifact,

the Washington Clock, by Jean-Baptiste Dubuc, portrays four essential themes: accountability —

the clock; the nation's first president — General Washington; the nation's totem — eagle; and the

---

[1] William Francis Butler, *Charles George Gordon by Colonel Sir William F. Butler*
(London: MacMillon and Company, 1892), 85.

[2] David Hackett Fisher, *Washington's Crossing* (Oxfrod: Oxford University Press, 2004),
371.

[3] Ibid.

1

nation's motto — E Pluribus Unum. All of which not only embody the American way of life but also the American way of war.

The essence of the American way of war is the natural outcome of the interaction between domestic politics, national values, and military experiences. This interaction is not a new phenomenon within civilizations. Yet, it was the eighteenth century Prussian military theorist and philosopher, Carl von Clausewitz who set the foundation in which politicians, strategist, and military scholars alike can understand the essence of war, strategy, tactics, operational art, and politics. Clausewitz's asserts, "since war is not an act of senseless passion but is controlled by the political object, the value of this object must determine the sacrifices to be made for it in *magnitude* and also in *duration*."[4] Therefore, the domestic politics, national values, and military experiences, although not inclusive, encompass what Clausewitz calls the value of the object. The natural by-product of the American way of war is captured in a simple Clausewitzian formula: V (value of the object) = M (magnitude of effort) + D (duration).

To capture the nature and influence that domestic politics and the American way of war variables have on military operations, this monograph uses a two-clock metaphor. The first clock represents domestic politics (Washington clock) and the second symbolizes military action (theater clock). This metaphor makes it possible to gain useful insights into the important relationship between these two forces acting on the duration of military operations. Although current ideology and idioms indirectly mention the impact of the Washington clock, contemporary doctrine fails to account for the constraint of the Washington clock on conducting and planning for military employment.[5]

---

[4] Carl von Clausewitz, *On War*, Indexed, ed. Michael Howard and Peter Paret, trans. Michael Howard and Peter Paret (Princeton, NJ: Princeton University Press, 1976), 94.

[5] 60 Minutes, September 30, 2012. During a 60 Minute TV special, General Allen alluded to the fact that time, specifically dates set by the elites drives theater planning, particularly how U.S. forces redeploy out of Afghanistan.

A thorough examination of the Vietnam War illustrates the utility of the clock metaphor, and more importantly, the relationship between domestic politics and operational art. This analysis also demonstrates the dynamic interaction that politics and operational art has on campaign planning and designing the operational approach. Historians, political scientists, and practitioners of military art and science have studied both the discourse and the narrative of politics and its relationship with the conduct of war.[6] This monograph seeks to build upon this body of knowledge through a scaling lens of campaigns and operations associated with the Vietnam War from 1955 to 1975. When viewed through the combined lenses of politicians, historians, theorists (military and political scientists), and senior military leaders, in concert with Untied States Army doctrine, the friction between war and politics comes to life. Clausewitz describes this interaction of war and politics: "[a]s policy becomes more ambitious and vigorous so will war... Policy is guiding intelligence and war the only instrument, not vice versa," thus war becomes subordinate to politics.[7] This subordination thrusts upon military planners the responsibility to plan within the constraints of the Washington clock. The construct of the Washington clock and theater clock is a useful way to understand that the relationship between domestic politics and the design of military campaign plans. The goal of this monograph is to illuminate this relationship and to show that ignoring the existence of the two clocks increases operational risk to mission and personnel, reduces tactical opportunities, and increases the risk of strategic failure.

---

[6] For additional perspectives on the relationship between politics, strategy, and war, see the following: Thucydides, *The Landmark Thucydides: A Comprehensive Guide to the Peloponnesian War* (New York: Free Press, 1998). Don M. Snider and Suzanne C. Nielsen, *American Civil-Military Relations: The Soldier and the State in a New Era* (Baltimore: The Johns Hopkins University Press, 2009). Samuel P. Huntington, *Changing Patterns of Military Politics* (New York: The Free Press of Glencoe, Inc, 1962). Joseph Nye's works on the uses of smart, hard, and soft power; and Christopher O' Sullivan, *Colin Powell: American Power and Intervention from Vietnam to Iraq* (Maryland: Rowman & Littlefield Publishers, 2009).

[7] Clausewitz, 94.

THE CLOCKS

Q: General, you talked about a Baghdad clock and a Washington clock. Can you explain what you mean by that?

GEN. PETRAEUS: Yeah, sure. You know, what I [have] said is that there [is] a Washington clock ticking — and actually, to be fair to those in Washington, it [is] an American clock. And — but that clock is moving, and it [is] moving at a rapid rate of speed.[8]

— General David Petraeus, CENTCOM Commander

In order to understand the clock metaphor, a brief analysis of the clock's origin and its very nature of time keeping are important. Clocks fall into three main functional groups: mechanism, function, and style. These three main categories are sub-classified as quartz or pendulum. Quartz clocks are instruments designed to maintain accuracy of time regardless of variations in temperature, motion, humidity, or air pressure. The efficacy and accuracy of the pendulum clock is dependent on the ability to keep the clock stationary, thus minimizing the motion or acceleration of the pendulum. As closed systems, digital and quartz clocks have the capability to function regardless of external factors. Conversely, pendulum clocks are open systems and external factors influence the performance of its function, consequently requiring adjustments to the counterweights in maintaining momentum. To depict both the unpredictability and rationality of war, the Washington and theater clocks are best thought of as pendulum clocks. The justification for choosing a pendulum clock metaphor is quite simple. It has several inputs both internal and external that influence the speed at which the clocks move. A pendulum is a rod anchored at a fixed point, with a bob attached to the free end that swings back and forth. This system appears to be simple and static. However, by virtue of the many internal and external inputs that can shape the speed of the clock it exhibits many of the behaviors of a complex system

---

[8] David General Petraeus, *DoD News Briefing with Gen. Petraeus from the Pentagon*, April 26, 2007, http://www.defense.gov/transcripts/transcript.aspx?transcriptid=3951 (accessed September 3, 2012).

— much as war itself does.[9]A detailed discussion of these components and its relationship to Clausewitz's construct of war follows in the upcoming section.

The simplicity and elegance of the pendulum clock reside in interaction with the dial, the period, the weight, and the power gears. The dial, the face of the clock, is the most visible element of pendulums. Yet, the period (amount of time it takes the pendulum to move over an arc one time) and the bob (mass at the end of the rod or chain) are what fascinate infants and scientists alike. Something as novel as Newton's Cradle or Foucault's Pendulum still captures the attention of many.

Figure 2. Newton's Cradle.

Source: Created by Author

In fact, Galileo observed that the pendulum's swing remains constant regardless of the amount of mass exerted upon it. Galileo further deduced that the only variable that affects the period is the length of the pendulum.[10] The weight and the power gears generally believed to play a larger part in the physics of a pendulum, play a secondary role. This secondary role deals with the basic

---

[9] The pendulum, invented by Christiaan Huygens, played an integral role in the development of western science, cultures, and society. Its origins date back to the seventeenth century and multiple studies by Galileo Galilee, Isaac Newton, and Robert Hooke. However there are two distinct types of pendulum clocks. The first is an Invar Pendulum (Riefler) and the other is Shortt clock. The Riefler clock because of the invar reacts to the change of temperate, routinely achieved a time-interval uncertainty for about ten (10) millisecond per day. Whereas the Short clock operated with two pendulums, one as slave and the other synchronized electrically to another pendulum. This reduced the uncertainty to one (1) millisecond per day.

[10] $[T = 2\Pi \sqrt{(l/g)}]$ The T equals the time, l equals the length, and g equals the gravity.

mechanics of the potential energy that is stored (weight) the interaction of the power gears and falling weight to drive the clock mechanism (dial) at the correct speed.[11] The dial depicts the time, while gravity and the power gears create equilibrium and momentum.

The only tangible variable that can affect the period (rate of speed) of the pendulum is the length of the rod or chain. Therefore, in order to affect the tempo (duration) of an operation, the length of the rod must increase or decrease. The bob of the pendulum clock represents metaphorically what Clausewitz calls the magnitude of effort. Although not directly related to effecting the period, using the bob's potential energy and Law of Conservation Energy, the magnitude of effort is directly equal to the bob's potential energy. Which means, the more the magnitude of effort the increases, the greater the probability and potential for the pendulum to swing without intervention.

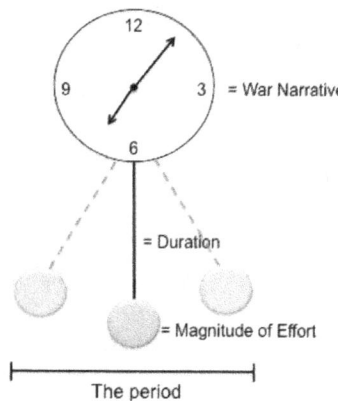

Figure 3. The Pendulum Metaphor.

Source: Created by Author; the overall system (clock) represents the value of the object.

---

[11] This phenomenon is explained in the Law of Conservation of Energy, which is described in the dynamics of the pendulum clock: the longer a clock runs, then more energy it uses and a heavier weight can store more potential energy. Therefore, theoretically, it could run longer than one with a lighter weight, thereby indirectly making the bob a critical component in timekeeping. Establishing the basic mechanics of the pendulum clock shows how the clock's components are just as dynamic in the Washington clock.

The theoretical underpinning of this monograph relies on Clausewitz's discussion of how much effort to expend. His answer is that the value of the political object dictates the effort, which is then measured in both magnitude and duration. When the effort exceeds the value of the object, the object must be renounced and peace must follow. The Washington clock illustrates the relationship between duration and magnitude of a military enterprise in pursuit of a political object. An integral concept in understanding the value of the object is its story and its storytellers. The storytellers, the military and political elites construct the value of the object through a war narrative. The war narrative becomes a causal story and problem representation that constructs the specific stakes identified and favors war. If the war narrative substantially changes, the value of the object and the operation of the Washington clock can change as well. The Washington clock as described in this study represents the war narrative.[12]

The war narrative also must support the normative and cognitive legitimacy of the war policy. Normative legitimacy is about the cost, (in blood and in treasure) and the stakes (risk), as well as values (culture, artifacts, etc.). Specifically, if the values are not commensurate with how the war is fought, then it (war) loses legitimacy, which is an essential character of the United States' war narrative. President's Johnson's comment that if "he lost Walter Cronkite he had lost Mr. Average Citizen", is an illustration of the importance of normative legitimacy.[13] Cognitive legitimacy is about feasibility, which is the notion that military effort accomplishes the outcome(s). The operational artists' understanding of both the environment and the problem indirectly affects the war narrative, thus affecting the duration and the value of the object. Therefore, if the war policy appears to be effective, then there is no change, subsequently

---

[12] Kubiak, Jeffrey J., *Battle on the Home Front: Elite Debate and the American National Will in War*, (PhD diss., Tufts University, 2010).

[13] Max Boot, *The Savage Wars of Peace, Small Wars and the Rise of American Power* (New York: Basic Books, 2002), 309.

validating the cognitive legitimacy and sustaining the normative legitimacy. It is for this reason that senior military leaders feel the need to demonstrate results. In the case of the Vietnam War, commanders and staff created metrics to chart success. The Vietnam War measured success in enemy body counts whereas Operation Iraqi Freedom (OIF) and Operation Enduring Freedom (OEF) chose a less macabre measurement of the frequency of Improvised Explosive Devices detonation and the number of schools constructed. Because of this, the value of the object, the war narrative, and the magnitude of effort are critical components that the operational artist must know and understand.

By analyzing the historical record of the Vietnam War, planners can understand the relationship between the Washington clock and theater campaign planning. Although synchronization of the two clocks is not entirely within the control of the operational artist, understanding how the clock operates and identifying the indicators early in the planning process can mitigate both the operational and the strategic risk. Using an abstract framework the clock metaphor illustrates that there are variables that relate directly to the domestic political context of a war and theater planning that operational planners can either control or influence.

The Washington Clock

The Washington clock has two independent variables and one dependent variable that incorporate the four basic components of a pendulum clock: the dial, the period, the weight, and the power gears. The independent variables included the inner workings and the length of pendulum. The dependent variable is the speed of the clock — the rate at which the clock approaches expiration. Underneath the dial (the war narrative) consists of the clock's inner workings — the power gears. Each gear represents the key components of the war narrative: the war policy, the national will, and the elites (political and military).[14] The war narrative, in of

---

[14] Throughout this monograph, national will encompasses national values and popular

8

itself, does not represent an isolated, prescriptive, or static story. In fact it is made up of a conglomerate of stories that are fluid in its movement (narration) and evolve as well as devolve over time and space. Ultimately the war narrative becomes the visible symbol of values, ideals, and artifacts that are easily recognizable. The fundamental role played by the war narrative is to construct the stakes, costs, and expectations of war policy. In this metaphor, the dial represents war narrative.[15] The second component of the war narrative, the national will, is the political sustainability of United States' policy. It seeks to satisfy foreign policy objectives predominantly with military force — or war policy.[16]

Yet, there is a direct correlation between the amount of reaction from the American public and war policy. Clausewitz asserts that the lack of reaction from the people relates to the size and importance of the either the strategic aims or military objectives. In order for the elites to further an agenda, they must tell a causal story to stimulate the masses.[17] Therefore, the national will does not have to be stronger than the war narrative to affect the overall value of the object. The dynamics and interaction from the public reflects how the elites shape the war narrative and the war policy.

In fact political scientist, Dr. Adam Berinsky claims, "it is reasonable to think that political leaders — those actors with the most at stake in a given controversy — would make such

---

support demonstrated by statics and polls.

[15] The dial, specifically the hands, become the indicators that tactical actions, arranged in time, space, and purpose are approaching the rational limit of duration established by the inner workings of the war narrative. The closer the hands reached twelve o'clock.

[16] Kubiak, 28.

[17] Throughout American history the amount of fervor originating from the masses varies on the incident or the indignation caused by an unprovoked attack. In the nineteenth century, it was the sinking of the USS Maine that furthered the Spanish-American War agenda. In the twentieth century, it was the attack on Pearl Harbor that turned U.S. apathy towards England into a declaration of war. In the twenty-first century, it was the simultaneous attacks on September 11th that launched U.S. into a two-front war.

calculations. In this conception the events of war are important, but only acquire explanatory power indirectly", that "(t)he public in the aggregate appears 'rational' only because they take cues from elites who sensibly incorporate diplomatic actions and events on the battlefield into their decisions to support or oppose war." [18] For that reason, elites will continue to play a crucial role in the implementation of the war policy, crafting the narrative, and stirring national will. Because the value of the object is abstract in nature, and its construction the product of a complex system of domestic politics, no simple metric exists to identify with any precision its exact value at any time. However, the operational artist need only to have a general idea as to the actual value of the object, but must pay close attention to changes in its value. On this point, public opinion serves as a useful, albeit crude, operationalization of changes in the value of the object.[19]

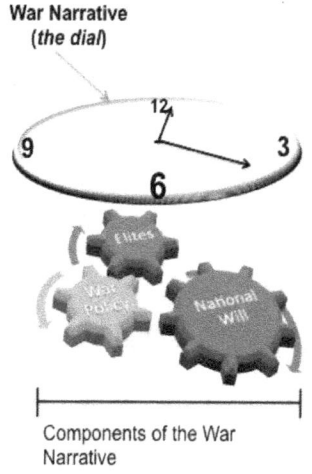

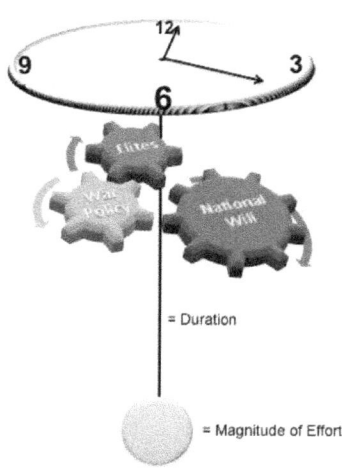

Figure 4. The inner workings.

Source: Created by Author

Figure 5. The Washington clock.

Source: Created by Author; the major components of the overall system

[18] Adam J. Berinsky, "Assuming the Costs of War: Events, Elites, and American Public Support for Military Conflict," *Journal of Politics* 69, no. 4 (2007), 981.

[19] Berinsky, *Silent Voices: Public Opinion and Political Participation in America* (Princeton: Pinceton University Press, 2005).

The war narrative carries the discourse between elites regarding the normative and cognitive legitimacy or illegitimacy of the war policy.[20] Normative legitimacy explains the desirability of a war policy whereas the cognitive legitimacy establishes the war policy's feasibility. Normative and cognitive legitimacy are interdependent and interconnected — and in that event highly susceptible to change. This change can be gradual over an undetermined period and "…need not be caused by a large-scale event."[21] Therefore, the value of the object, the war narrative, magnitude of effort, and duration directly affects how the operational artist employs military forces in time, space, and purpose.

The Theater Clock

The theater clock is less scientific than the Washington clock and more of an abstract metaphor. Although similar in its design as a pendulum clock, the theater clock serves to illustrate that war cannot be a mindless driver of policy. Subsequently, responsibility lies in how the operational artist frames the environment, understands the problem, and designs the operational approach. The operational artist's knowledge of how the Washington clock and the operational approach are interrelated and interdependent affects the campaign plan. For that reason, the theater clock is the application of operational art, which is the pursuit of strategic objectives, in whole or in part, through the arrangement of tactical actions in time, space, and purpose.[22] The positioning of the bob on the pendulum (the length of the rod) becomes the essence of the

---

[20] Alexander George, "Domestic Constraints on Regime Change in U.S. Foreign Policy: The Need for Policy Legitimacy," in *American Foreign Policy: Theoretical Essays* (New York: Longman, 2002), 322.

[21] J. L. True, B. D. Jones and F. R. Baumgartner, "Punctuated-Equilibrium Theory," in *Theories of the Policy Process*, ed. Paul A Sabatier, 155-88 (Boulder: Westview Press, 2007), 160.

[22] Department of the Army, *ADP 3-0, Unified Land Operations* (Washingtion: Government Printing Office, 2011), 9.

11

operational approach. The art lies in the operational artist's ability to design an operational approach that slows down the clock and reduces risk. The war narrative illustrates the importance of the value of the object; it determines the resources and the acceptable risk (magnitude of effort). While, the amount of time (duration) shapes the operational approach, and frames the operational environment.

It is through the theater clock metaphor that the operational artist gains insight into the relationship between the war narrative, the value of the object, the magnitude of effort, and duration. It is here that a causal story emerges within the war narrative. This 'if' and 'then' correlation deals primarily with the two dependent variables. If the value of the object (outcome) changes, an adjustment in resources and/or time must occur in order to maintain stability within the narrative. The Vietnam War case study shows that the war narrative altered with each executive and legislative administration. This variance occurred because the value of the object changed and the desired outcomes were not attainable. Essentially, the war lost its cognitive legitimacy. The success or failure of a military operation in theater in achieving its objectives influences the domestic political arena's perception of cognitive legitimacy of the war narrative. In order for the value of the object to remain stable and therefore the resources and time to remain stable, the operational artist must show cognitively that military effort achieves the political objectives. This forces congruence and synchronization with both the Washington clock and the theater clock. Within the framework of the theater clock, two causal relationships become essential to planning: (1) show results; (2) manage perceptions and expectations.

Consideration one, show results or progress. If progress cannot be shown, then the narrative is affected (indirectly), time becomes more of a constraint, and the operational planner's understanding of the operational environment is either incorrect or incomplete. Thus, behavior in theater shapes the perception of the narrative's legitimacy back in the domestic political arena. To avoid this pitfall, the artist needs to understand the war policy and its players. The first realization is that, the war policy frames and sets the desired outcome for wars. This same war policy is also shaped by the political and military elites' debate and perception. The product of this discourse assigns a value to the object. The war policy becomes part of the war narrative's master-plot. The storyline describes the cost and whether or not military action is effective.

Consideration two, manage perceptions and expectations. It is here that the operational artist needs to link the ways (operational approach) with the Washington clock and the war narrative. If her understanding of the operational environment is not congruent with war policy then she is undermining the war narrative. The relationship between the cognitive legitimacy and the operational approach rests upon the argument that the set of problems presented in the war are amenable to a solution by military force. The Vietnam War (early 1960 to the late 1960) illustrates what happens when military forces do not show progress nor manage perceptions or expectations. In fact a "longstanding criticism of democracies, but especially the American democracy, is that Americans are impatient. They want to see success sooner than later. This was a criticism that people levied against United States during World War II, indeed though out."[23]

Summary

This monograph seeks to explore the relationships between domestic politics and operational art. Paramount to the stability of the war narrative is the synchronization of the clocks. Using this mental-model the operational artist gains a better understanding of the operational environment, identifies the problem and designs the operational approach. The artist must then look for opportunities and reduce risk by staying aligned with or ahead of the Washington clock. During the Vietnam War, Secretary of Defense Robert McNamara correctly perceived that the Washington clock was going to expire before the theater could justify the military effort, validate the campaign plan, yield substantial gains, or achieve the political

---

[23] *Timeline of War's Progress Differs in U.S., Kabul*, NPR, September 14, 2009.

objectives. An analysis of the Vietnam War in its entirety, 1950 to 1975, uses the theoretical

principles introduced in this section to answer the research question: what is the relationship

between the Washington clock and theater campaign planning? The remainder of this monograph

highlights the multiple narratives spanning five US administrations, the volatility and instability

of the war narrative, the relationship of the cognitive and normative legitimacy with the value of

the object, and the incongruence of the Washington and theater clock.

THE VIETNAM WAR FROM 1955 to 1975

Basically, as far as Vietnam is concerned, we won practically all the battles but, by any sensible definition of strategic objective, we lost the war. This is a new experience — harrowing, sorrowful, but true. Thus, it [is] absolutely imperative that we study how it is that you can win so frequently, and so well, in a war — fighting sense, and yet lose a war in a strategic or political sense. It [is] unique; and it [is] not something that we want to duplicate.[24]

— Major General DeWitt Smith, July 1977

The genesis of the United States involvement in the Vietnam War originated in 1955 with President Dwight Eisenhower who pledged America's support to the South Vietnamese President Ngo Dinh Diem and his struggle against communist residing within the country. Eight years later President Kennedy expanded U.S. involvement by announcing: "we want the war to be won, the Communists to be contained, and the Americans to go home. But we are not there to see a war lost".[25] Kennedy's statement became the American war policy that shaped the early years of the U.S. role in the Vietnam War. It also explains why the Vietnam War's narrative oscillated between the rhetoric of both World Wars and the Korean War. Unlike many other U.S. wars, Vietnam did not have a unifying catastrophic event that shaped the war narrative. It became a war of just enough, but not too much. This gradualism initially enabled the clocks to operate independently. Because of the incongruence of the clocks and the change in the war narrative the Vietnam War is an ideal case study to demonstrate the clock metaphor's usefulness. First, it illustrates the tension created when the Washington clock does not start or is slower than the theater clock. Secondly, it demonstrates the tactical and operational outcomes when the theater

---

[24] The BDM Corporation, *The Strategic Lessons Learned in Vietnam Omibus Executive Summary* (McLean: Department of the Army, 1980), Ex-1.

[25] *The Pentagon Papers: The Defense Department History of United States Decisionmaking on Vietnam*, The Senator Gravel ed. (Boston: Beacon Press, 1971). v2, 828.

clock stays ahead of the Washington clock. Lastly, it reveals the problems that occur when the Washington clock forces the theater clock to speed-up.

The primary focus of this section is the application of operational art that illustrated the relationship of the two clocks. This section comprises four major distinct sub-sections. The first subsection, the Vietnam War from 1955-1964 ~ Limited Partnership, explores the historical background and United States' advisory role. It will also frame the dominant war narrative, the value of the object, magnitude of effort, as well as the strategic aims. Subsection two, the Vietnam War from 1965 to 1968 ~ Americanization, frames the evolving war narrative and provides strategic context before analyzing key tactical actions of that period. These key tactical actions — Operations SILVER BAYONET, CEDAR FALLS, and JUNCTION CITY — show the dynamics of the two clocks. The third subsection, the final years of the Vietnam War from 1969 to 1975, follows the same general outline as subsection two. However, the analysis of the key tactical actions varies from those conducted during 1969 to 1975 ~ Peace with Honor. These tactical actions — Operation APACHE SNOW, Cambodia Campaign, and Operation LAM SON 719 — demonstrate the implications of changing the value of the political object, and the effect that has on the magnitude of the effort and duration of time allowed. Finally, Section III concludes with the 'so what' of the clock metaphors within the context of the entire Vietnam War.

Section II introduced the concept of the war narrative and its interaction with the other variables of the Washington clock. From 1955 to 1964, three presidents presided over the Vietnam War and each took a slightly different approach but the overall Vietnam War narrative, policy, and strategy remained largely the same. Their emphasis, U.S. was not to intervene directly in Vietnam.[26] The rationale was that political objectives must be limited because total war is not a

---

[26] The information that follows highlights the congruence amongst presidents' foreign policy narrative and strategy. (1) Presidents Dwight D. Eisenhower in 1954 "You have a row of

viable solution in a nuclear age. Thus, strategic and tactical aims must be limited in scope and approach. During this era, the United States was politically and militarily focused on European economic recovery, the success of the United Nations and the Marshall Plan. As a result, events in Southeast Asia became secondary and more of an economy of force, which shaped the value of the war.

The Vietnam War from 1955 to 1964 ~ Limited Partnership

While preventing the spread of communism was the dominant U.S. foreign policy narrative during the 1950s and early 1960s, the amount of resources put forth in Southeast Asia displayed what the elites considered the value of the object. The principals amongst the elites determining the U.S. Vietnam policy were the presidents. However, the amount of transparency amongst the political and military elites varied from administration to administration during the Limited Partnership phase of the Vietnam War. Eisenhower sought to keep the political and military informed as to minimize the possibility of a "sudden, unforeseen emergency". Conversely, Kennedy's distrust of the JCS minimized their influence within the decision-making process.[27] In contrast, Johnson skillfully provided the correct amount of suitable information need to gain consensus within the JCS and Congress. How these administrations viewed, the Vietnam

---

dominoes set up; you knock over the first one, and what will happen to the last one is that it will go over very quickly". (2) President John F. Kennedy in 1961, "Let every nation know, whether it wishes us well or ill, that we shall pay price, bear any burden, meet any hardship, support any friend, oppose any foe to the survival and the success of liberty". (3) President Lyndon B. Johnson in 1964, "If I left [the war in Vietnam] and let the Communists take over South Vietnam, then I would be seen as a coward and my nation would be seen as an appeaser, and we would both find it impossible to accomplish anything for anybody anywhere on the entire globe."

[27] During the Kennedy Administration, Kennedy recalled General Maxwell Taylor from retirement to serve as his special military representative. This moved signaled the level of distrust Kennedy felt towards the JCS.

problem framed both their policy and operational approach.[28] The first example of such was U.S. actions following the French withdrawal in 1954.

After the remainder of French military forces departed Vietnam, the United States filled that void by becoming the lead agent for economic aid and military advisors to the South Vietnam Government. The United States Military Assistance Advisor Group (USMAAG) began training and advising the Armed forces of the Republic of Vietnam (ARVN).[29] Nevertheless, by only sending 324 military advisors, the U.S. revealed its level of commitment to the war and relationship between the value of the object and the magnitude of effort.[30] The value of the object and the war narrative remained stable until February 1960, when MAAG received authorization to increase its personnel strength from 342 to 685. To reestablish American resolve the NSAM (National Security Action Memorandum) 52 reaffirmed that the policymakers desired outcomes in South Vietnam. The outcomes included: "prevent communist domination of South Vietnam; to

---

[28] *The Pentagon Papers: The Defense Department History of United States Decisionmaking on Vietnam:* v4, *v.* As noted in the *Pentagon Papers*, the elite debate from 1955-1964 "saw the development of the consensus on military pressures against the North and the decision to defer them for temporary reasons of tactics. The last quarter of 1964, the Johnson Administration recognized that some type of "overt pressures mounting in severity against North Vietnam soon would be required." The justification for these pressures was twofold: degrade the will and capabilities of DRV to force Hanoi to rescind their support for the war in the South; and to induce negotiations at some future point in time on our terms after North Vietnam has been hurt and convinced of our resolve. To achieve this, DRV must believe three things: one, the U.S. was taking limited action to achieve limited goals; two, the U.S. commitment was total; and three the U.S. had established a sufficient domestic consensus to see the policy through.

[29] The MAAG involvement in Vietnam began as early as 1952. Their original charter started with supporting the French military effort, to include reorganizing and training armed forces of South Vietnam, Laos and Cambodia. From 1955 to 1960, the MAAG chiefs (LTG John W. O'Daniel and LTG Samuel Williams) focused their efforts in developing a South Vietnam forces capable of defeating a conventional invasion.

[30] Neil Sheehan, Fox Butterfield, Hendrick Smith and E. W. Kenworthy, *The Pentagon Papers: The Secret History of the Vietnam War* (New York: Quadrangle Books, 1971), 92-97. The Department of Defense was apprehensive to undertake this effort. The JCS feared that the advisory limit imposed by the Geneva Accords (342 military personnel) was too restrictive to permit a successful training program.

create in that country a viable and increasingly democratic society; and to initiate, on an accelerated basis, a series of mutually supporting actions to achieve this objective."[31] Along these lines, a significant change in value of the object and subsequently in the magnitude of effort did not occur until the spring of 1961, when President Kennedy authorized the increase of the MAAG from 685 personnel to 2,285 in addition to deploying 400 Special Forces to serve specifically as counterinsurgency advisors to the South Vietnamese military.[32] This marked a transitional period where the concept of a "flexible response" became the war policy. It would not be until late 1964 that the policy again changed the magnitude of effort, this time to reflect a conventional approach. By the spring of 1964, the magnitude of effort jumped exponentially from 2,285 personnel to 23,300 military personnel.[33]

General Maxwell Taylor, as Kennedy's special envoy to evaluate the military and political situation in Vietnam, recommended that the U.S. transition beyond the indirect approach of a hands-off advisor role to a more engaged method as an active military partner.[34] The direct approach required the deployment of thousands of additional forces. In addition to an increase of forces Taylor recommended: "a change in the charter, the spirit, and the organization of the MAAG in South Vietnam...from an advisory group organization to something nearer — but not

---

[31] McGeorge Bundy, National Security Action Memorandum No. 52, May 11, 1961, in The National Archives [The Collection of JFK- National Security Files, 1961-63], http://research.archives.gov/description/193451, (accessed February 1, 2013).

[32] Sheehan, 92-97. May 1, 1961 Memo, R. L. Gilpatric for Presidential Task Force.

[33] Congressional Quaterly, *China and U.S. Far East policy, 1945-1967* (Washington, D.C.: Congressional Quaterly Service, 167), 170.

[34] Graham A. Cosmas, *MACV The Joint Command in the Years of Escalation, 1962-1967* (Washington, DC: Center of Military History, 2006), 18.

quite — an operational headquarters in a theater of war."[35] Kennedy agreed with him and made the changes, thereby increasing the U.S. commitment to South East Asia.

The third component of the war narrative, national will and popular support, played a role in determining the value of the object and the magnitude of effort during the Vietnam War's formative years. The data available from U.S. opinion polls taken in the late 1950s and early 1960s suggests that the American public were not very concerned with military events in Vietnam.[36] For that reason, as seen in Figure 6 and Table 1, public support for or against policies and strategies in Vietnam initially only had a negligible effect on the war narrative during the Limited Partnership phase. The lack of importance in the national will along with a waning war policy contributed to the Washington clock not operating until the fourth quarter of 1964.

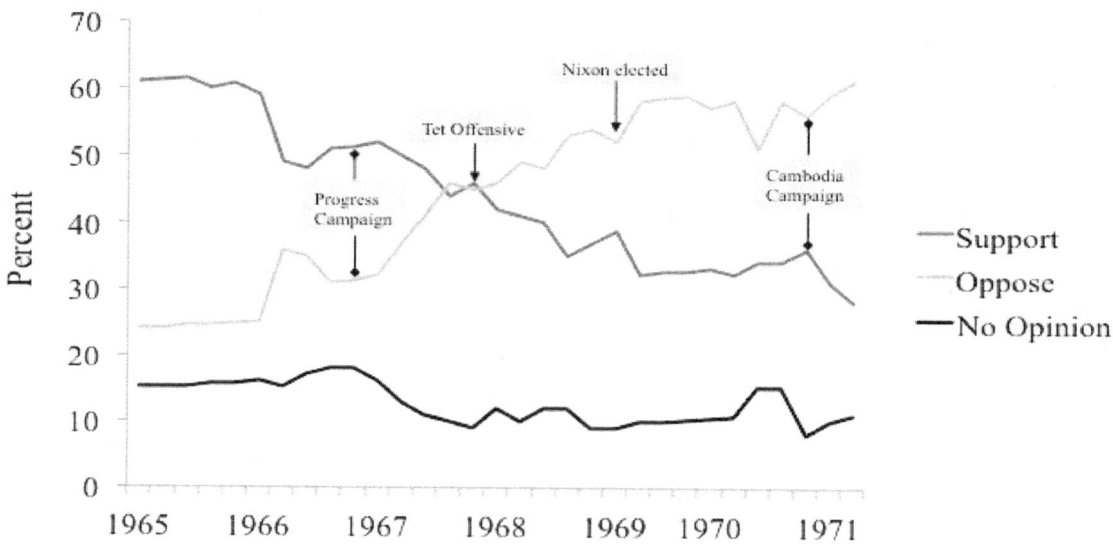

Figure 6. Trends in the American domestic support and opposition of the Vietnam War.

Source: Created by Author; data originated from John E. Muller's *War, President and Public Opinion*, 54-55.

---

[35] Ibid, 20.

[36] John E. Mueller, *War, President and Public Opinion* (New York: John Wiley & Sons, Inc, 1973), p 116.

20

Table 1. Popular reasoning for the Vietnam War

Survey question: Below are a list of arguments that were used for U.S. military effort in Vietnam. Review the question carefully, and then decide which of the two or three of the argument that are the strongest ones.	
Percentage	Reason
49	1. If we do not continue, the Communist will take over and then move on the other parts of the world
48	2. We must support our fighting men
33	3. If we quit now, it would weaken the will of other countries to defend their freedom
33	4. If we give up, the whole expenditure of American lives and money will have been in vain
24	5. The United States should never accept defeat
23	6. If we do not continue, we will lose prestige and the confidence of our confidence of our friends and allies abroad
19	7. We are committed to South Vietnam
14	8. If we pull out and the Communist take over, they will kill many of the Vietnamese who have opposed them
8	9. If we preserve, we are to gain our objectives

Source: Created by Author; data and questions originated from John E. Muller's *War, President and Public Opinion*, 49.

As a result of the Washington clock barely moving due to the lack of interest by the wider domestic political audience in the U.S., the MAAG operational artists had wide latitude in how they developed their campaign plan. It was here that the artist could plan without the constraints of time as to how to effectively deal with the National Liberation Front (NLF) and what Clausewitz calls a partisan war: an unconventional and internal war.[37] Using the strategy of gradualism and the military resources available during 1955 to 1964, operational artist designed a counterinsurgency theory and doctrine to address the operational environment and problem in Vietnam. The overarching concept was a limited partnership in which Taylor envisioned U.S. role as "friends and partners — not as arms-length advisors — [and] show them how the job might be

---

[37] The NLF is also known as the VC or Vietcong.

done — not tell them or do it them."[38] Yet, the conceptual planning of limited partnership did not yield the desired results and needed an overarching directive. As a result the National Security Action Memorandum (NSAM 288) issued on March 17, 1964 incorporated two new approaches: revive the pacification effort; establish a contingency plan involving direct U.S and South Vietnamese attacks on North Vietnam with the purpose of compelling Hanoi to cease its support of the Viet Cong.[39]

The Vietnam War from 1965 to 1968 ~ Americanization

The era from 1965 to1968, known as Americanization, brought about significant changes to the inner workings of the Washington clock. Within the war narrative, the value of the object and magnitude of effort under went some fundamental changes. Beginning as a simple advisory role with limited partnership in planning, military actions evolved into the U.S. taking direct intervention actions. While it began as a Vietnam problem with a Vietnam solution, the war quickly transitioned to a Vietnam problem with a distinctly American solution. This shift in strategy to Americanization produced an increase in the magnitude of effort. As additional resources increased so did the media coverage, debates amongst the elites, and popular concern for the war effort.

From 1965 to 1968, the MACV demonstrated success and the catalyst to change the war narrative did not occur until 1968. Once the magnitude of effort increased to include the major employment of combat forces, the Washington clock's rate of speed increased. By agreeing to send the 173rd Infantry Regiment and the 9th Marine Expeditionary Brigade to Vietnam in 1965,

---

[38] Department of Defense, *The Pentagon Papers - U.S.-Vietnam Relations, 1945-1967* (n.p.: Grotto Pulp Fiction, 2010-02-13), Kindle Locations 16190-16191.Amazon Kindle Edition.

[39] McGeorge Bundy, National Security Action Memorandum No. 288, March 17, 1964, in the National Security Action Memorandums (NSAMs) [Johnson Administration, 1963-69], http://www.fas.org/irp/offdocs/nsam-lbj/index.html (accessed February 1, 2013).

the administration signaled a change in the value of the object.[40] Exemplified in a statement made in the Pentagon Papers: "[d]ifference with respect to preparation for coping with enemy reactions to harsher pressures centered around the issue of committing greater numbers of U.S. ground forces to South Vietnam. CINCPAC, supporting General Westmoreland's request, urged provision for deployment of Marine and Army units to provide security for U.S./GVN operating bases".[41] The Vietnam War was now on the Washington clock — and it would never be the same.

The spring and summer of 1965 brought the arrival of seventeen combat units and new strategy predicated on enemy attrition.[42] However, MACV could not arrange those U.S. forces in time and space to accomplish the command's new operational approach, search and destroy. Once sufficient basing was established in theater, Westmoreland launched Operation SILVER BAYONET in the Central Highlands of South Vietnam. The three-day operation commenced on November 14, 1965 in II Corps Tactical Zone's (CTZ) Pleiku Province.[43] The battle damages assessment (BDA) of SILVER BAYONET, commonly known as the Battle of Ia Drang, included over 1,711 enemy causalities and 240 U.S. causalities.[44] These seemingly positive operational outcomes had major implications on how the MACV designed future operations. The SILVER

---

[40] Cosmas, *MACV The Joint Command in the Years of Escalation, 1962-1967*, 157-180.

[41] *The Pentagon Papers: The Defense Department History of United States Decisionmaking on Vietnam*: v4, 38.

[42] Cosmas, *MACV The Joint Command in the Years of Escalation, 1962-1967*, 204. Combat units referenced in this monograph are battlion size formations. The formation breakdown at the end of the summer of 1965 was thirteen Army battlaions and four Marine battalions.

[43] See Map 1 in Appendix A. To better, arrange units within South Vietnam, the MAAG and GVN portioned South Vietnam into four corps tactical zones. Each zone is responsible for security and stability and has a major population city.

[44] Hal Moore and Colonel Hieu, *LZ X-Ray After Action Report LTC Hal Moore and Colonel Hieu*, September 01, 2008, http://www.generalhieu.com/lzxray_moore_hieu-2.htm (accessed December 11, 2012).

BAYONET's kill ratio of 12 – 1 greatly contributed to Westmoreland's decision to fight and win

a war of attrition. Westmoreland couched the success of SILVER BAYONET to elites as the

archetype of how the U.S. would end this war, but he required additional resources.

By the end of 1966, MACV's troop strength increased to 389,400.[45] With strong basing

operations, decisive points identified, and a recognition that the strategic and operational hub of

Hanoi's power was its army, MACV launched two operations spanning the first two quarters of

1967.[46] Operation CEDAR FALLS, a three-week tactical engagement involved seventeen U.S.

maneuver battalions and five ARVN maneuver battalions. The military objectives of CEDAR

FALLS were to destroy the VC base areas twenty-five kilometers northwest of Saigon. This

three-phase operation began on January 6, 1967 had elements of the 25th Infantry Division

deployed with the primary task to block and a secondary task to search and destroy the local

enemy units and bases. The second phase (January 8th) included an air assault to secure then

search Ben Suc. The third phase (January 9th) consisted of an armored attack to cut the "Iron

Triangle" in half in order to facilitate the northern encirclement of the objective by air assault.[47]

Operation CEDAR FALLS' BDA: 750 enemy casualties, and 72 U.S. causalities, a 10 – 1 kill

ratio. With such unbalanced BDA assessment, surely it was only a matter of time before the

MACV would compel Hanoi to cease its support for the Viet Cong.

MACV launched a series of operations in February with the purpose of maintaining

pressure on the enemy, the pattern of gradualism intended to communicate to the DRV the gravity

---

[45] Congressional Quaterly, 170.

[46] *The Pentagon Papers; the Defense Department History of United States Decisionmaking on Vietnam:* v4, v or National Security Action Memorandum No 288. Reports and presidential envoys during the Kennedy and Johnson administration stated that the war would end if Hanoi felt enough pressure and sustained enough causalities.

[47] Bernard W. General Rogers, *Cedar Falls-Junction City: A Turning Point* (Washington, D.C.: Government Printing Office, 1989), 15-24, 30-34.

of the situation. Operation GADSTON began on February 2, 1967 in War Zone C, achieved minor results. The night patrol and ambushes of Operation FAIRFAX on the outskirts of Saigon in III CTZ were successful, as enemy activities within the area noticeably declined. On the other hand, the operation that had the greatest impact during the month of February was Operation JUNCTION CITY. It commenced on February 22, 1967 with an airborne assault into enemy sanctuaries in II CTZ's northern Tay Ninh Province.

After eighty-two days of offensive tactical actions focused on the elimination of the VC, MACV units cleared the VC out of the northern Saigon region. Much like General George Washington in the American War of Independence, Westmoreland understood the fact that he needed to act decisively whenever possible — and constantly give the appearance of positive action regardless of the individual outcomes of battles or campaigns. Westmoreland's new strategy of attrition, using the body-count metric, allowed the MACV to demonstrate measurable progress, which in-turn allowed the MACV to stay ahead of the Washington clock for the time being. Such ideas were predicated upon the acceptance of the basis that after "operations like JUNCTION CITY and CEDAR FALLS were completed, the VC would have few places left to hide within the boundaries of the South Vietnam."[48] Thanks to the measured rate of progress in the form of body counts, captured weapons and terrain held (however temporary), the military elites in Vietnam and Washington believed that this direct military intervention could be completed in two-half years. The only caveat was the MACV needed additional troops. The increase in resources applied and the perception of improved operational success prompted more optimistic expectations in the U.S. and was the impetus for the Washington clock to tick a little faster in order to catch-up with the theater clock.

---

[48] Department of Defense, *The Pentagon Papers - U.S.-Vietnam Relations, 1945-1967* (n.p.: Grotto Pulp Fiction, 2010-02-13), Kindle Locations 20411-20415. Amazon Kindle Edition.

The request for additional troops sent by Westmoreland on April 5, 1967 created friction back in the domestic political arena with Johnson administrations and Congress.[49] Senators believed that "we [Congress] should give our military leaders more support (presumably troops) and we should hit North Vietnam harder (notably in Haiphong)."[50] The political pressure continued to mount against the Johnson administration as Senator John C. Stennis proselytized that Congress should meet Westmoreland's request "even if it should require mobilization or partial mobilization."[51] Stennis also stated that the MACV was "100,000 men shy of the total needed to contain the Viet Cong militarily."[52] Despite Stennis' strong rhetoric, some elites were apprehensive about the notion of having U.S. forces in Vietnam for two-half years regardless of the size. Using the same body count metric to demonstrate progress, the rising opposition to the Vietnam War believed that 1,194 (144 KIA and 6 MIA) U.S. causalities produced by Operation CEADR FALLS in one week, seemed counterintuitive to ending the war.[53] The possibility of suffering 1,194 casualties per week for the next two-half years provided enough validation for critics that the cost in blood might be too great.[54] It is in this relationship that the inner workings

---

[49] Cosmas, *MACV The Joint Command in the Years of Escalation, 1962-1967*, 416. For the detailed MACV justification of this request, see Ltr, Westmoreland to CINCPAC, 5 Apr 67, sub: FY 68 Force Requirements, with appendixes and annexes, in CMH files.

[50] Department of Defense, *The Pentagon Papers - U.S.-Vietnam Relations, 1945-1967* (n.p.: Grotto Pulp Fiction, 2010-02-13), Kindle Locations 40272-40273. Amazon Kindle Edition.

[51] Department of Defense, *The Pentagon Papers - U.S.-Vietnam Relations, 1945-1967* (n.p.: Grotto Pulp Fiction, 2010-02-13), Kindle Locations 40274. Amazon Kindle Edition.

[52] Sheehan, 536-538.

[53] Department of Defense, *The Pentagon Papers - U.S.-Vietnam Relations, 1945-1967* (n.p.: Grotto Pulp Fiction, 2010-02-13), Kindle Locations 40281. Amazon Kindle Edition.

[54] Ibid. Conversely a substantial number of the American people seemed to believe that political restraints imposed upon our military leaders were the chief cause of so little concrete progress. This belief and the potential untapped political support it revealed, was to be a powerful lever in the hands of the JCS as they pressed for force increases during Program 5.

of the Washington clock were primed to spin the hands of the war narrative even faster, and possibly either change the course of the war or the end of the war.

By early 1968, the war narrative had reached something of a tipping point. It is also the same span when the operational artist had the greatest impact on the U.S. war policy in Vietnam by indirectly affecting the normative and cognitive legitimacy of the war narrative. This snapshot in time commenced with a nationwide offensive by the VC during the Tet Holiday of 1968 with a battle in South Vietnam's ancient city Hue as the biggest assault of the '68 Tet Offensive. The multi-phased 213 – day offensive resulted in 45,000 NVA/VC KIA and 1,000 U.S. KIA. Despite the 45 – 1 kill ratio and an operational defeat for the NVA/VC, Westmoreland's MACV were deemed the loser of the conflict on the U.S. and international stage. One of the starkest catalysts was photojournalist Eddie Adams' photograph of South Vietnamese General Nguyen Ngoc Loan executing a Viet Cong prisoner in Saigon, February 1, 1968. This graphic portrayal by the media highlighted the atrocities during the '68 Tet Offensive and created uproar within the domestic and political arena. During Westmoreland's Progress campaign, he couched the enemy as not only being incapable but also severely attrited. So how was it possible that a third rate country could launch a nationwide offensive if they were losing? How could the U.S. support a regime with such depraved indifference to human life and due process? These questions filled the media airways and plagued Mr. Citizen's thoughts. The MACV won the '68 Tet Offensive but lost the cognitive and normative legitimacy.[55]

---

[55] The Tet Offensive also created cognitive dissonance within the U.S. domestic political atmosphere because Westmoreland and the Johnson administration had just finished running a determined "Progress" campaign to convince the domestic audience that the massive investment in Vietnam was worth it and that there was light at the end of the tunnel. In the wake of the Tet Offensive, the American public and the elites doubted and mistrusted the administration. After all, if the perception of winning and making progress demonstrated in MACV's body-count metrics how was it that the NVA/VC could launch a nationwide offensive within SVN?

To further perpetuate the ineffectiveness of how the war was being conducted and whether or not this war could have be won, world-renowned journalist, Walter Cronkite, reported his first-hand observation of the Vietnam War:

> To suggest we are on the edge of defeat is to yield to unreasonable pessimism. To say that we are mired in stalemate seems the only realistic, yet unsatisfactory, conclusion. On the off chance that military and political analysts are right, in the next few months we must test the enemy's intentions, in case this is indeed his last big gasp before negotiations. But it is increasingly clear to this reporter that the only rational way out then will be to negotiate, not as victors, but as an honorable people who lived up to their pledge to defend democracy, and did the best they could.[56]

Sensing that he might be running out of time, Westmoreland, on March 18, 1967 requested a surge of 200,000 in addition to the 470,000 currently deployed in order to break the enemy's resolve.[57] In spite of this, Johnson pressured by his advisors as well as public opinion opted not to support the full request of the senior military commander. During his March 31, 1968 address to the nation, Johnson explained, "[s]o tonight, in the hope that this action will lead to early talks, I am taking the first step to deescalate the conflict. We are reducing — substantially reducing — the present level of hostilities."[58] This denial for additional troops marked the shift in both the political and military strategy and the war narrative. What had been an Americanized search and destroy strategy became a strategy of pacification and Vietnamization.

This change in war policy affected the operational artist application of operational art throughout the remainder of 1968 to 1969. One example was the Battle of Khe Sahn. The attack on Khe Sahn started on January 21, 1968 by NVA and continued as 179-day siege. Recognizing

---

[56] February 27, 1968 CBS broad cast by Walter Cronkite (Reporting Vietnam: Part One: American Journalism 1959-1969 (1998), pp. 581-582)

[57] Cosmas, *MACV The Joint Command in the Years of Escalation, 1962-1967,* 416.

[58] Transcript from LBJ library President Lyndon B. Johnson's Address to the Nation Announcing Steps To Limit the War in Vietnam and Reporting His Decision Not To Seek Reelection March 31, 1968 source http://www.lbjlib.utexas.edu/johnson/archives.hom/speeches.hom/680331.asp (accessed December 11, 2012).

the similarities in France's plight during the Battle of Dien Bien Phu, Westmoreland monitored the situation closely — in his mind, Khe Sahn could not fall.[59] The Marines sustained heavy casualties and their only source of resupply was via air. Eventually the Battle of Khe Sahn was abandon, highlighting the perception amongst Vietnam veterans that those who died did so for nothing.[60] Another blow to the credibility of the cognitive legitimacy occurred in November 1969 when the cover-up of the My Lai massacre surfaced, demonstrating that the artist has the potential to indirectly change the value of the object by undermining the cognitive and normative legitimacy. The era of 1965 to 1968 started out with the theater clock operating ahead of the Washington partly because MACV demonstrated success and partly due to both the Johnson administration and elites believing that what Vietnam needed was a military solution not a political solution. The Americanization era started with the theater clock ahead, but it ends with the synchronization of the clocks and the Washington clock accelerating.

The Vietnam War from 1969 to 1975 ~ Peace with Honor

The Peace with Honor period, from 1969 to 1975, reveals what happens when the Washington clock not only surpasses the theater clock, but also forces it to speed up. During this era, the inner workings of the Washington clock changed both the war narrative and the value of the object. To analyze the events and military actions from 1969 to1975, it is necessary to examine the "political situation in the United States and the peace negotiations in Paris in order to

---

[59] Some believed that Khe Sahn was America's Dien Bien Phu, where the collapse of Dien Bien Phu became the impetus to drive France out of Vietnam. With the elite discourse and civil unrest, Johnson could not afford to lose Khe Sahn. As a result, he requested to have sand table constructed and hourly updates throughout the duration of the siege.

[60] This is a reason why US withdrawals from Afghanistan and Iraq are carefully planned, deliberate, and publicized. Hew Strachan argued that Afghanistan and Iraq lasted longer not to achieve to the desired end state but to ensure that those who have died did not do so in vain.

29

properly contextualize Vietnamization within U.S. strategy in South Vietnam."[61] The hands of time were ready to spin and the Nixon administration placed more constraints on the operational artists forcing them to keep pace while balancing the risk to the strategic objects and troops.

Change to the United States' Vietnam strategy finds its roots in 1968 during the presidential campaign. The candidates, Richard Nixon and Vice President Hubert Humphrey, both ran on 'end the Vietnam War' platforms. Once Richard Nixon won the 1968 election, he maintained his predecessors' overall foreign policy approach of containment. The continuation of this grand strategy, and his desire to end the war with honor, shaped the war narrative and the value of the object for the remainder of the Vietnam War.

Nixon's plan to end the war included the following six goals. First, reverse the Americanization of the Vietnam War that occurred from 1965 to 1968 and focus instead on Vietnamization. Next, give more priority to pacification so that the South Vietnamese could better able to extend their control over the countryside. Then reduce the threat of invasion by destroying enemy sanctuaries and supply lines in Cambodia and Laos, while simultaneously the withdrawing half a million American troops from Vietnam in such a manner that would not bring the collapse of South Vietnam. The fifth goal focused on negotiating a cease-fire and a peace treaty. Lastly, demonstrate U.S. willingness and determination to stand by the South Vietnamese President Nguyễn Văn Thiệu if the peace agreement was violated by Hanoi, and assure South Vietnam that it would continue to receive our military aid as Hanoi did from its allies, the Soviet Union and, to a lesser extent, China.[62]

By the end of 1969, MACV saw its first reduction in troop strength from a peak of 536,100 to 475,200. This 60,900 decline reflected a decline in the value of the object as exhibited

---

[61] James H. Willbanks, *Abandoning Vietnam, How America Left and South Vietnam Lost Its War* (Lawrence, KS: University Press of Kansas, 2008), 2.

[62] Richard Milhous Nixon, *The Real War* (New York: Warner Books, 1980), 106.

in the public opinion.[63] Operational artist decisions in Vietnam did not alleviate the political and

domestic tension. For example, Operation APACHE SNOW (aka Hamburger Hill), a ten-day

joint operation, commenced May 10, 1969. Similar to Operation CEDAR FALLS, APACHE

SNOW was deemed an operational success with a BDA scoring 630 NVA/VC KIA and 56 U.S.

KIA.[64] Despite the 10 – 1 kill ratio, any American casualties sustained after four years of fighting

generated turmoil and protest amongst the elites and, as seen in Figure 6, a continued decline in

public opinion. According to scholar and historian Lewis Sorley, the Nixon administration

desperately needed time to "institute the new policy, and Nixon, desirous of achieving 'peace

with honor', had to make sure there were no more Hamburger Hills. As a result he sent word to

Abrams to take measures to hold down U.S. causalities."[65]

Another indication that the Washington Clock was accelerating ahead of the theater clock

came in the summer of 1969 in the form of budget reductions with a twenty-two percent cut in the

B – 52 fleet and other sorties.[66] Subsequently, MACV's reduced capability to respond to multiple

contingencies with massed firepower increased the strategic and operational risk. In a

memorandum to Wheeler, Abrams conspicuously stated that in order to mitigate the risk and for

---

[63] See Figure 6. Mueller, 55. Polls taken during September 1969 and Janurary 1970, the adminstration's conduct of the Vietnam War recvied its third lowest approval rating with thirty-three percent in favor of the war and fifty-seven against the war.

[64] 101st Airborne Division, "After Action Report, Battle of Dong Ap Bia," reprinted on Congressional Record, 91st Cong., 2nd session., 116 (29 December 1970): S210403; Col Joseph B. Conmy, "I Led a Brigade at Hamburger Hill," Washington Post, 27 May 1989. One of the most comprehensive narratives of the Battle of Dong Ap Bia, or Hill 939, is Samuel Zaffiri, Hamburger Hill, May 11-20, 1969 (Novato, Calif.: Presidio Press, 1988).

[65] Lewis Sorley, Thunderbolt, General Creighton Abrams and the Army of His Time (Bloomington: Indiana University Press, 2008), 261.

[66] Shaw, 30 or message from Gen Wheeler CJCS to Gen Abrams COMUSMACV, 260126Z March 1970, Subject: Plan for ground strikes against base camps in Cambodia, Abrams Papers, CMH Histories Division. "Higher authority" meant President Nixon. See also Webb, Joint Chiefs of Staff and the War in Vietnam, 131-160.

the Vietnamization process to succeed while U.S. presence in SVN decreased, MACV needs to maintain an airmobile reserved.[67] The combination of troop decrease and reduction in air power demonstrated that the value of the object was decreasing and the speed of the Washington clock was steadily increasing. If reductions in troops were going to continue and U.S. planned to end the war with honor, the military strategy needed to change.

In an address to the nation on November 3, 1969, Nixon outlined his exit strategy for the Vietnam War. He called this strategy Vietnamization and it was his way to slow the Washington Clock down.[68] Nixon stated that the Vietnamization program required phasing in South Vietnamese forces while phasing out American forces. According to Nixon, this "phasing out will save American lives and cut American costs."[69] Hence, Abrams, the operational artist, had to quickly prepare the RVNAF to fill the void left by redeploying U.S forces.[70] Abrams sought to find a way to balance "combat capability and much capability for as long as possible."[71]

In order to do so, Abrams began to reframe the environment and the problem. He concluded that the familiar problem had changed; Hanoi's approach morphed into "a blend of political and military activity calculated to achieve anti-war pressure in the U.S. leading to a rapid redeployment of U.S. forces, the collapse of the GVN, and the creating of a coalition government

---

[67] Ibid.

[68] The term was coined during the Johnson administration under Clark Clifford in 1968, but Nixon adopted and publicized it as his solution to ending the Vietnam War.

[69] Willbanks, 7.

[70] Willbanks, 48 and Henry Kissinger, *White House Years*, 276. Abrams assume command in July 1968 and received a change of mission on August 15: 1) provide maximum assistance to strengthen the armed forces of South Vietnam; 2) increasing the support to pacification effort; 3) reducing the flow of supplies to the enemy down the Ho Chi Minh Trail.

[71] Ibid.

in SV."[72] Anticipating that the MACV needed more time to implement Vietnamization, understanding that causalities were no longer palatable to the American public, and seeing an acceleration of the reduction of resources, Abrams directed a small group of personnel to draft contingency plans to achieve the strategic aims during the winter of 1970.

On the evening of March 25, 1970, Abrams officially received a directive from Nixon to design a plan that would achieve U.S. strategic objectives: validation of Vietnamization and deliberate withdrawal of U.S. forces.[73] To accomplish this, MACV recommended to the Nixon administration that the allies maintain pressure on the enemy's lines of communication along the Cambodia-South Vietnam border. Abrams' ability to plan quickly relied on his acknowledgment of the speed of which the Washington clock was operating and his situational understanding of the operational environment. Abrams, also correctly framed the problem: MACV must plan for and conduct a corps level attack while simultaneously withdrawing from the theater of operations and maintaining the cognitive and normative legitimacy of the new American policy of peace with honor. Simultaneously to MACV's planning efforts, the political elite in Washington debated war narrative and war policy. Vice President Agnew bluntly framed the problem within the elite debate: "Either the sanctuaries were a danger or they were not. If it was worth clearing them out, [Agnew] did not understand all the pussyfooting about the American role how what we accomplished by attacking only one [Fishhook and Parrots Beak]. Our task was to make Vietnamization succeed."[74] However, Secretary of Defense Melvin Laird's chief concern was that

---

[72] Shaw, 30 or message from Gen Abrams to ADM McCain CINPAC and Gen Wheeler CJCs, 131133Z March 1970, subject: Force planning, Abrams Papers, CMH Histories Division.

[73] Ibid, 31 and Graham A. Cosmas, *MACV The Joint Command in the Years of Withdrawal, 1968-1973* (Washington, D.C.: Centers of Military History, 2006), 296.

[74] Shaw, 40 or Henry Kissinger, *Ending the Vietnam War: A History of America's Inovlvement in and Extrication from the Vietnam War* (New York: Simon & Schuster, 2003), 153-54.

the popular support would vociferously oppose anything they perceived as widening the war.[75] On April 28, 1970, and after much consternation, President Nixon authorized the Cambodia Campaign to commence on May 1, 1970.[76]

Attempting to re-establish normative and cognitive legitimacy for both the war and the Cambodia Campaign, Nixon held three press conferences during the spring and summer of 1970. The first was an unprecedented address to the nation held on April 30, 1970. Nixon briefed, in detail, the plan for the Cambodia Campaign. He also nested the tactical actions with the strategic purpose: "[t]o protect our men who are in Viet-Nam and to guarantee the continued success of our withdrawal and the Vietnamization programs."[77] The May 8th press conference, tailored specifically to address the normative legitimacy of MACV's actions was to reemphasize to the American public and the elites the temporary nature of the Cambodia Campaign. The June 30th media conference Nixon restated the four key points for the campaign:

1. North Vietnam had brought the war to Cambodia

2. NVA troops had continued to Sihanouk's downfall

3. Sihanouk's government and the Cambodian National Assembly had deposed Sihanouk;

4. A major NVA/VC base activity had led to action by the Americans and South Vietnamese, after allies had endured blatant violations of Cambodian neutrality for five years.[78]

---

[75] Ibid, 30.

[76] Ibid, 40 or Richard Milhous Nixon, The Memoirs of Richard Nixon (New York: Warner Books, 1978), 448-51.

[77] Gerhard Peters and John T Woolley, *Richard Nixon: Address to the Nation on the Situation in Southeast Asia. April 30, 1970*, The American Presidency Project, http://www.presidency.ucsb.edu/ws/?pid=2490 (accessed March 5, 2013).

[78] Shaw, 155 or Hal Kosut, *Cambodia & the Vietnam War*, (New York: Facts on File,

Maintaining the narrative of the Vietnam War, MACV and the Nixon administration needed to demonstrate the feasibility of the new war policy. Kissinger stated that the Vietnamization strategy measure of effectiveness resulted in the reduction of U.S. casualties: "in the twelve months before Cambodia, more than 7,000 Americans had been killed in action. In the year after, the figure was less than 2,500. The next year [1972] it fell to less than 500."[79] Regardless of the reductions in fatalities as the result of the Cambodia Campaign, Nixon mandated that MACV would not operate outside the borders of South Vietnam.[80]

After successfully slowing the Washington clock down to allow for the safe withdrawal of American forces, Abrams and the GVN required a vehicle to demonstrate the cognitive legitimacy of the policy and that peace with honor were achievable. Thus, ARVN needed to take lead in a major combat operations and Operation LAM SON 719 became that opportunity. In February 1971, the ARVN I Corps, supported by American airpower, conducted a limited offensive into Laos. MACV wanted the attack to demonstrate that the ARVN had enough offensive capability to disrupt the lines of communication of the NVA and protect its borders. The forty-five day operation resulted in the loss of 700 American rotary assets, the death of sixty-six American crewmembers, 160,000 sorties flown by allied forces and 9,775 (3,800 killed, 5,200 wounded, and 775 missing) ARVN causalities.[81] Ultimately, LAM SON 719 delayed a major invasion from NVA into South Vietnam for thirteen months and allowed the withdrawal of U.S. ground combat forces from a position of strength not weakness. Nonetheless, it failed to produce

---

1971), 123.

[79] Shaw, 157 or Kissinger, *Ending the Vietnam War*, 175.

[80] Peters and Woolley, http://www.presidency.ucsb.edu/ws/?pid=2490 (accessed March 5, 2013).

[81] Willbanks, 111-116.

the long-term operational effects needed to bring about enduring strategic change. The strategic failure of LAM SON 719 showed the limitations of the Vietnamization strategy.

By the spring of 1972, U.S. troop strength reverted to Limited Partnership era of 95,000, of which only about 6,000 were combat troops.[82] With the continued withdrawal of troops and upcoming presidential election year, Hanoi assumed that domestic political pressures in the U.S. would preclude Nixon from stopping the withdrawal and adding new forces. That assumption became the impetus for PAVN's attack across the DMZ into II CTZ's Central Highlands, coined the Easter Offensive of 1972. Nixon responded with aggressive bombing campaigns called LINEBACKER I and LINEBACKER II.[83]

By the beginning of 1973, U.S. combat death toll was 58,082. The Nixon administration's LINEBACKER campaigns provided enough pressure on Hanoi to compel them to return to the negotiation table. Subsequently, all parties involved signed the peace treaty on January 27, 1973, ending U.S. military involvement in the Vietnam War. On December 12, 1974, North Vietnam launched a new offensive into South Vietnam and established a foothold within South Vietnam's I CTZ and II CTZ.[84] President Gerald R. Ford, opted not to honor Nixon's promise to provide air support, did not respond to South Vietnamese President Nguyễn Văn Thiệu request for assistance, and offered little diplomatic pressure against Hanoi. On April 30, 1975, North Vietnam and the NLF forces entered Saigon. The last U.S. government personnel embarrassingly evacuate the embassy from the rooftop by helicopter as depicted in the Dutch

---

[82] George C. Herring, *America's Longest War: The United States and Vietnam, 1950-1975*, Thrid (New York: McGraw-Hill, Inc, 1996), 271.

[83] Guenter Lewy, *American in Vietnam* (New York: Oxford University Press, 1978), 411. LINEBACKER I and LINEBACKER II lasted for 179 days, 43,776 sorties flown, expended 175,918 tons of bombs over 75,000 square miles killing a 100,000 North Vietnamese.

[84] Herring, 340. The Battle of Phuoc Long between NVA and GVN lasted twenty-five days and resulted in approximately 3,160 (1,600 KIA) South Vietnamese casualties and 1,300 NVA/VC causalities.

photojournalist, Hubert van Es famous photo, *The Fall of Saigon*.[85] Within four hours, the North Vietnam forces arrived at the abandoned embassy and declared the end of the Vietnam War.

Summary

This section opened with an epitaph from MG Smith that epitomized what Clausewitz described as strategy and its scale and effort: "the degree of force that must be used against the enemy depends on the scale of political demands on either side. These demands, so far as they are known, would show what efforts each must make; but they seldom are fully known..."[86] The strategies of attrition and Vietnamization in addition to the scale and effort put forth during the U.S. Vietnam War resulted in the deployment 550,000 troops, thousands of aircrafts flown, $150 billion dollars spent, and 58,213 casualties. Instead of mobilizing, calling up the reserves, whipping up patriotic zeal, successive U.S. administrations saw the environment and problem differently. Foreign policy expert, Leslie H. Gelb stated that each U.S. president and administration involved "essentially played the role of brakemen...Each did only what was minimally necessary at each stage to keep Vietnam and later South Vietnam out of Communist hands."[87] Whatever the policy and strategy called for, the means available tended to dictate and influence the operational artist's approach.

This conflict began under President Eisenhower, expanded under President Kennedy, grew in both scale and effort under President Johnson, sensationalized under President Nixon, and abated under President Ford. The Vietnam War demonstrated the strain between what the war

---

[85] Hubert van Es originally described this photograph as the evacuation of U.S personnel from a CIA building http://en.wikipedia.org/wiki/File:Saigon-hubert-van-es.jpg (accessed March 5, 2013).

[86] Clausewitz, 583-585.

[87] Leslie Gelb, "The System Worked," *Foreign Policy*, Summer 1971: 88-100.

policy called for versus what was actually done in theater.[88] Such frustration was eloquently described by Taylor who stated that, "it [Vietnam War] was never difficult to decide what should be done but it was almost impossible to get it done, at least in an acceptable period of time."[89] When viewed in its entirety, the Vietnam War more than any other war illustrates the tension created when the Washington clock does not start, demonstrates what happens when the theater clock stays ahead of the Washington clock, and highlights the tension created when the Washington clock forces the theater clock to speed-up. The art becomes how the operational artist synchronizes the two clocks.

---

[88] Robert William Komer, *Bureaucracy Does its Thing: Insitutional Constraints on U.S.-GVN Performance in Vietnam*, DARPA (Santa Monica: The RAND Corpoartaion, 1972), 8

[89] Komer, 8.

CONCLUSION

No one starts a war rather, no one in his senses ought to do so without first being clear in his mind what he intends to achieve by that war and how he intends to conduct it. The former is political purpose; the latter its operational objective. This is the governing principle which will set its course, prescribe the scale of means and effort which is required, and makes its influence felt down to the smallest detail.[90]

— Carl von Clausewitz, Prussian Military Theorist

"And in one year," I [McChrystal] continued, "we'd better demonstrate progress — something that we said was going to happen, happened — or political support, left and right, will evaporate."
Jeff Eggers, a brilliant SEAL whom the chairman had allowed me to pluck form his strategic advisory group, put the matter of time to me starkly in a dead-on assessment that I [McChrystal] read that week: "This campaign may not end for a decade, but it will be decided within a year."
As we flew east toward the war, clocks were ticking.[91]

— General Stanley A. McChrystal, ISAF Commander

This monograph examined the relationship between the Washington clock, its inner workings, and theater campaign planning. Though never explicitly stated in any body of knowledge whether it is academia or military doctrine, the rate at which the Washington clock moves directly influences the operational artist campaign plan. This study's intention was to identify and describe the phenomenon, understand its mechanics and interaction with campaign planning, and then examined a historical campaign using the two-clock metaphor. The dynamics of the Washington clock and theater campaign planning show the three salient features required to understand the operational environment. First, the war policy equates to the use of military force in order to achieve a political objective. The value of the object is constructed in the war narrative, which has normative (desirability) and cognitive (feasibility) components. Lastly, the

---

[90] Clausewitz, 579.

[91] General Stanley A McChrystal, *My Share of the Task: A Memoir* (New York: Penguin Group, 2013), 291.

value of the political object determines both the magnitude of effort and time (demonstrated in the equation: $V = M + D$). The Washington clock also represents the time that the war policy is given before it is changed by a waning narrative or an agreement by the elites that the level of effort has exceeded the value of the object.[92]

The mental model presented in this study helps the operational artist frame the environment and the problem. As one of the operational artist during the Americanization period, General Lewis W. Walt fell prey to the lack of situational awareness and situation understanding. As the III Marine Amphibious Force commander, Walt stated: "[s]oon after I arrived in Vietnam it became obvious to me that I had neither a real understanding of the nature of the war nor any clear idea as to how to win it."[93] Thus, the operational artist must understand the value of the object in order to design a campaign plan.

This conclusion examines the usefulness of the two-clock metaphor in framing the operational environment and the operational problem. It will also identify what contemporary conflicts illustrate the phenomenon and three basic relationship used to analyze the Vietnam War: the Washington clock has not started; the theater clock is ahead of the Washington clock; and the Washington clock forces the theater clock to speed up.

<u>The Washington Clock Has Not Started ~ OEF-P</u>

Currently, Joint Special Operations Task Force (JSOTF-P) has approximately 600 U.S. personnel deployed to the Philippines in a strictly non-combat role to advise and assist the Armed Forces of the Philippines (AFP), share information, and to conduct joint civil military operations.[94] Due to

---

[92] Solving the above equation for time a new formula emerges: D=V/M.

[93] Komer, 1.

[94] JSOTF-P Public Affairs, "Joint Special Operations Task Force – Philippines Fact Sheet," *JSOTF-P*, July 1, 2011, http://jsotf-p.blogspot.com (accessed February 28, 2013). U.S. committed twenty-four million dollars to over two hundred humanitarian projects from October

its size, funding, mandate, and casualties to date it would not be a far stretch to make parallels with the Vietnam War's Limited Partnership era.[95] Because OEF and OIF were competing for resources, efforts in the Philippines became an economy of force. Thus tension between the magnitude of the effort and the value of the object did not exist. The cost in blood and treasure when compare to effort in Afghanistan and Iraqi during the same timeframe were less than one percent. As a result, the constraint of time plays less of a role for JSOTF-P allowing OEF-P to continue as a war in the periphery.

Currently OEF-P receives little if any mention in both written and visual medias. As long as the cost in blood and treasures remains low, JSOTF-P maintains the normative and cognitive legitimacy, and sensational attacks originating out of the Philippines on American soil or interest, the Washington clock will not start. U.S. Embassy Spokesperson, Lee McClenny alluded to the fact that the JOSTF-P is having a significant impact in training the AFP and light reaction company (LRC) with search and destroy mission in the archipelagos. He also asserted that the thirty-two million dollars per year to support approximately 500 to 600 U.S. personnel which is the equivalent of about five hours of operation in Iraq.[96] This low threshold allows the theater clock's pendulum to swing without interference from external variables.

2007 to June 2011 in Task Force Mindanao's area of responsibility. USAID contributes approximately eighty million dollars per year in the Philippines. This is less than one percent of the OIF and OEF effort. Organized and deployed in February 2002 as part of the Balikatan Exercise, JSOTF-P consists of three geographically located task forces: Task Force Archipelago, Task Force Mindanao, and Task Force Sulu. Balikatan is a Tagalog phrase, which means shoulder-to-shoulder. This exercise started in 1981 as a bilateral exercise between the U.S. and GRP. However, Balikatan 2002 provided the U.S. and GRP to conduct rescue operations and search and destroy missions on the island of Basilan

[95] Operations conducted in support of OEF-P from 2002 to 2009 resulted in the lost 15 U.S. personnel assigned to JSOTF-P. Data pulled from *icaualities.org* and Joint Special Operations Task Force (JSOTF-P) website.

[96] Max Boot and Richard Bennet, "Treading Softly in the Philippines," *The Weekly Standard*, January 5-1222-28, 2009.

<u>The Theater Clock is Ahead of the Washington Clock ~ OEF-Afghanistan (2001-2009)</u>

In a more contemporary vignette rife with speculation and criticism, significant shifts in both the value of the object and the magnitude of effort have shaken things up for U.S. forces in Afghanistan. With rhetoric inundating the media regarding the United States military posture post 2014, inference as to the remaining *value* of staying in Afghanistan can hardly be avoided.[97] Perhaps the most publicized illustration of the change to both the value of the object and the war narrative was President Barrack Obama's December 1, 2009 address to the nation. During his speech, Obama stated that Afghanistan regressed and that the status quo was no longer sustainable. Therefore, he authorized the deployment of an additional 30,000 troops for 2010.[98] However, the International Security Assistance Force commander, General Stanley A. McChrystal requested 80,000 troops to stop the regression and maintain regional stability.[99] The delta of 50,000 troops and change to the war policy reflected the emerging tension between the Washington and theater clocks. . Yet, up until the fall of 2009, the theater clock was ahead showing small gains and reasonable amount of success. However as the war in Iraq began to draw down gradually, the embolden insurgents in Afghanistan started to regain their foothold within Regional Commands East and South area of operations. The end of 2009 not only brought about a

---

[97] *Timeline of War's Progress Differs in U.S., Kabul*, NPR, September 14, 2009. A very pointed observation from a non-elite, Rene Montagne: "We being this morning with Afghanistan and a story about two clock. One ticks in Washington, the other in Kabul. They measure progress in the war. The challenge: They are moving at very different speeds."

[98] Barack H. Obama, "Remarks by the President in Address to the Nation on the Way Forward in Afghanistan and Pakistan," *www.whitehouse.gov*, December 1, 2009, http://www.whitehouse.gov/the-press-office/remarks-president-address-nation-way-forward-afghanistan-and-pakistan (accessed April 3, 2013). A summarization in McChyrstal's book *My Share of the Task*, 359-361.

[99] McChrystal, 332. Although McChrystal states in his memoir that he requested an additional 40,000 troops a myriad of media sources (New York Times, CBS News, ABC News, CNN, etc.) state that the 40,000 increase was the middle option with 80,000 as the high option in the ISAF commander's August strategic assessment report.

change in the value of the object, the magnitude of effort, and duration, it also significantly increased the speed of the Washington clock. The theater clock is behind and remains so today.

The Washington Clock Forces the Theater Clock to Speed-Up ~ OIF (2006-2008)

A common observation made during the Vietnam War is frequently valid during OIF: "Whatever the policy called for, it simply was never tried on any major scale until 1967-1971." For example, the U.S. input into the highly publicized Strategic Hamlet Program during the Americanization phase of the war was farcically small. Conversely, U.S. marginal efforts during stability operations in Iraq achieved limited results. An over reliance on measuring the measurable created a quantitative measurement system used to gauge military effectiveness and performance in order to demonstrate progress. This drove the operational planning process. Both the Iraq and Vietnam metrics were created to either measure: body counts, comparative kill ratios, weapons captured to weapons lost ratios, IED reduction and interdiction, frequency and accuracy indirect fire, patrols conducted, schools built, and security assistance training these became indicators of success. The measure of effectiveness and performance created the perception that U.S. was winning the counterinsurgency effort and with a little more pressure, (aka the surge) the violence will end.

As the operational artist, General David Petreaus understood the war narrative, the value of the object, as well as the existence and importance of the Washington and theater clocks. Operational artist also created ad hoc units and systems to address the unfamiliarity of the problem such as: Human Terrain Teams (HTT), Company Intelligence Support Teams (COIST), Money as a Weapon System (MAAWS), and commercial off the shelf equipment such as Mine-Resistant Ambushed Protected Systems (MRAPS), Combined Information Data Network Exchange (CIDNE), and Command Post of the Future (CPOF). Yet, events such as Abu Grab, Camp Bucca, and the Kill Company overshadowed OIF's quantitative metrics and innovative programs. These events affected the war narrative's cognitive and normative legitimacy.

With unexpected events such as the Kill Company, loss of elite support in the U.S. Senate during the 2006 election, and the American population's growing impatience with the ongoing war, the OIF war narrative changed.[100] Keenly aware of this sense of urgency, Petreaus stated that the "Washington clock is moving more rapidly than the Baghdad clock, so we [are] obviously trying to speed up the Baghdad clock a bit and to produce some progress on the ground that can, perhaps ... put a little more time on the Washington clock."[101] Subsequently, Petreaus requested additional troops and developed the foundation of a counterinsurgency strategy, which is now inoculated into U.S. Army doctrine.

The increase pace of Washington clock placed it significantly ahead of the theater clock during 2006 to 2008. This forced the operational artist to design operational approaches that slowed the pace of the Washington clock in order to allow the synchronization of the theater clock. OIF from 2006 to 2008 demonstrates the tension created when the Washington clock forces the theater clock to speed-up.

<u>Summary</u>

The operational artist normally understands the magnitude of effort variable because of its connection to the resources given. The artist also understands the duration variable when designing a campaign and arranging tactical actions in time space and purpose to accomplish the mission within the recommended temporal threshold. If the primary purpose of war is to achieve

---

[100] CBS Poll: "Talk First, Fight Later". CBS.com, 24 January 2003, http://www.cbsnews.com/2100-500160_162-537739.html, accessed on 8 September 2012. The January 2003 CBS public opinion survey concluded that sixty-four percent of Americans approved of military action against Iraq. Sixty-three percent of Americans wanted Bush to find a diplomatic solution rather than go to war, and sixty-two percent believed the threat of terrorism directed against the U.S. would increase due to war. In 2004, fifty-three percent approved of military action, a loss of thirteen percent. Two years later only forty-one percent approved of military action.

[101] Thomas E. Ricks, *The Gamble: General David Petraeus and the American Military Adventure in Iraq, 2006-2008* (New York: The Penguin Press, 2009), 148.

a position of relative advantage, then the critical variables of war become the value of which the opposing states place on their respective strategic aims, in relation to the price (blood and treasure) each state is willing to pay to accomplish their desired outcome. The artist must also be aware of her role in shaping changes in the value of the object by her influence on the normative (way the war is fought; setting expectations of what can be achieved with what costs) and cognitive legitimacy (showing results) of the war narrative. Once that change in the value in the object occurs the operational artists reframes the environment and problem in order to design an operational approach that reflects the change in either the duration or magnitude of effort.

Realizing the majority of models are inherently incapable of representing reality there are some models that are especially usefully, particularly for the American operational artists. Using this pendulum model, operational artist gain an in depth understanding of one of the most critical constraints — time. Understanding the operational environment and problem in order to design an operational approach that synchronizes the clocks is paramount for maintaining stability of the war narrative. The artist must look for opportunities and reduce risk by staying align or ahead of the Washington clock. McNamara, Abrams, McChrystal, and Petreaus correctly perceived that the Washington clock was going to expire before the theater could validate the military effort, validate the campaign plan, yield substantial gains, or achieve the political objectives. The Vietnam War case study from 1955 to 1975 illustrated these dynamics.

APPENDIX A: MAP

Map of MACV'S CTZS in Vietnam[1]

---

[1] Source: created by author, base map from Cosmas, *MACV The Joint Command in the Years of Escalation, 1962-1967*, 26.

BIBLIOGRAPHY

Barzun, Jacques. *From Dawn to Decadence: 500 Years of Western Culture Life; 1500 to Present.* New York, NY: Harper Collins, 2000.

Bello, Walden. "A 'Second Front' in the Phlippines." *The Nation*, March 18, 2002: 18-22.

Bennet, Richard, and Max Boot. "Treading Softly in the Philippines." *The Weekly Standard*, January 28, 2009.

Bennett, Alexander L. George and Andrew. *Case Studies and Theory Development in the Social Sciences.* Cambridge, MA: MIT Press, 2006.

Berinsky, Adam J. "Assuming the Costs of War: Events, Elites, and American Public Support for Military Conflict." *Journal of Politics* 69, no. 4 (2007).

—. *In Time of War: Understanding American Public Opinion from World War II to Iraq.* Chicago: University of Chicago Press, 2009.

—. *Silent Voices: Public Opinion and Political Participation in America.* Princeton: Pinceton University Press, 2005.

Beyerchen, Alan. "Clausewitz, Nonlinearity, and the Unpredictability of War." *International Security* (The MIT Press) 17, no. 3 (Winter 1992-1993): 59-90.

Boal, Michael. "The Kill Team: How U.S. Soldiers in Afghanistan Murdered Innocent Civilians." rollingstone.com. March 27, 2011. http://www.rollingstone.com/politics/news/the-kill-team-20110327#ixzz2N5J0l7lb (accessed February 9, 2013).

Boot, Max. *The Savage Wars of Peace, Small Wars and the Rise of American Power.* New York: Basic Books, 2002.

Bousquet, Antoine. *The Scientific Way of War.* New York, NY: Columbia University Press, 2009.

Brookes, Peter. "Flashpoint: No Bungle in the Jungle." *Armed Forces Journal.* September 2007. http://www.armedforcesjournal.com/2007/09/2926516/ (accessed March 10, 2013).

—. "The 'Frogoten Front' Should be Remembered." *China Post.* July 13, 2007. http://www.chinapost.com.tw/commentary/the-china-post/peter-brookes/2007/07/13/116149/The-'Forgotten.htm (accessed March 10, 2013).

Burke, John P. *Honest Broker? The National Security Advisor and Presidential Decsion Making.* College Stattion: Texas A&M University Press, 2009.

Butler, William Francis. *Charles George Gordon by Colonel Sir William F. Butler.* London: MacMillon and Company, 1892.

Calhoun, Mark T. "Clausewitz and Jomini: Contrasting Intellectual Frameworks in Military Theory." *Army History*, no. 80 (Summer 2011): 22-37.

Clausewitz, Carl von. *On War*. Indexed. Edited by Michael Howard and Peter Paret. Translated by Michael Howard and Peter Paret. Princeton, NJ: Princeton University Press, 1976.

Congressional Quaterly. *China and U.S. Far East Policy, 1945-1967*. Washington, D.C.: Congressional Quaterly Service, 167.

Cosmas, Graham A. *MACV The Joint Command in the Years of Escalation, 1962-1967*. Washington, DC: Center of Military History, 2006.

—. *MACV The Joint Command in the Years of Withdrawal, 1968-1973*. Washington, D.C.: Centers of Military History, 2006.

Department of Defense. *DOD National Defense Strategy*. June 2008.

—. Joint Publication (JP) 3-0, *Joint Operations* . Washington, DC: Government Printing Office, 2011.

—. Joint Publication (JP) 5-0, *Joint Operation Planning*. Washington, D.C.: Government Printing Office, 2011.

Department of Military Strategy, Planning, and Operations. *Campaign Planning Handbook*. Carlisle Barracks : United States Army War College , 2013.

Department of the Army. ADP 3-0, *Unified Land Operations*. Washingtion: Government Printing Office, 2011.

—. ADP 5-0: *The Operations Process*. Washington: Government Printing Office, 2012.

—. ADRP 3-0, *Unified Land Operations*. Washington, D.C.: Government Printing Office, 2012.

—. ADRP 5-0 *The Operations Process*. Washington: Government Printing Office, 2012.

—. ATTP 5-0.1 *Commander and Staff Officer Guide*. Washington: Government Printing Office, 2011.

—. FM 3-24, *Counterinsurgency*. Washington, D.C: Government Printing Office, 2006.

Dolman, Everell C. *Pure Strategy*. Abingdon: Frank Class, 2005.

Dueck, Colin. *Reluctant Crusaders: Power, Culture, and Change in American Grand Strategy*. Princeton, NJ: Princeton University Press, 2006.

Fisher, David Hackett. *Washington's Crossing*. Oxfrod: Oxford University Press, 2004.

Gelb, Leslie. "The System Worked." *Foreign Policy*, Summer 1971: 88-100.

General Petraeus, David. DoD News Briefing with Gen. Petraeus from the Pentagon. April 26, 2007. http://www.defense.gov/transcripts/transcript.aspx?transcriptid=3951 (accessed September 3, 2012).

General Rogers, Bernard W. *Cedar Falls-Junction City: A Turning Point*. Washington, D.C.: Government Printing Office, 1989.

George, Alexander. "Domestic Constraints on Regime Change in U.S. Foreign Policy: The Need for Policy Legitimacy." In American Foreign Policy: Theoretical Essays, by G. John Ikenberry. New York: Longman, 2002.

Herbst, Jeffery. *States and Power in Africa, Comparative Lesson in Authority and Control*. Princeton: Princeton University Press, 2000.

Herring, George C. *America's Longest War: The United States and Vietnam, 1950-1975*. Thrid. New York: McGraw-Hill, Inc, 1996.

Huntington, Samuel P. *Changing Patterns of Military Politics*. New York: The Free Press of Glencoe, Inc, 1962.

Huntington, Samuel P. "If Not Civilizations, What?" *Foreign Affairs*, 1993: 72-85.

JSOTF-P Public Affairs. "Joint Special Operations Task Force – Philippines Fact Sheet." JSOFT-P. July 1, 2011. http://jsotf-p.blogspot.com (accessed February 28, 2013).

Kalyvas, Stathis N. *The Logic of Violence in Civil War*. Cambridge: Cambridge University Press, 2006.

Khatchadourian, Raffi. "The Kill Company". TheNewYorker.com. 2009 йил 6-July. http://www.newyorker.com/reporting/2009/07/06/090706fa_fact_khatchadourian (accessed February 9, 2013).

Kissinger, Henry. *Ending the Vietnam War: A History of America's Inovlement in and Extrication from the Vietnam War*. New York: Simon & Schuster, 2003.

—. *White House Years*. New York: Simon & Schuster Paperbacks, 2011.

Komer, Robert William. *Bureaucracy Does its Thing: Insitutional Constraints on U.S.-GVN Performance in Vietnam*. DARPA, Santa Monica: The RAND Corpoartaion, 1972.

Kosut, Hal. *Cambodia & the Vietnam War*. Edited by Hal Kosut. New York: Facts on File, 1971.

Kubiak, Jeffery J. "Battle on the home front/Elite debate and the American national will in war." dissertation, Tufts University, 2010.

Lawrence, Mark Atwood. *The Vietnam War War: A Concise International History*. Oxford: Oxford Universoty Press, 2008.

Lewy, Guenter. *American in Vietnam*. New York: Oxford University Press, 1978.

Magnuson, Stew. "Forgotten Front." *National Defense*, February 2008: 48-51.

49

Major General Chiarelli, Peter W., and Patrick R Major Michaelis. "Winning the Peace, The Requirement for Full-Spectrum Operations." *Military Review*, 2005: 4-17.

Maslowski, Peter and Millett, Allan R. *For the Common Defense, A Military History of the United States of America*. New York: The Free Press, 1994.

Maxwell, Colonel David S. "Operation Enduring Freedom: What would Sun Tzu Say." May-June 2004: 20-23.

McChrystal, General Stanley A. *My Share of the Task: A Memoir*. New York: Penguin Group, 2013.

McDougal, Walter *A. Promise Land, The American Encounter with the World since 1776*. New York: Houghton Mifflin Company, 1997.

McGreal, Chris. "Kill Team: US platoon commander guilty of Afghan murders." guradian.com. 2011 йил 10-November. http://www.guardian.co.uk/world/2011/nov/11/kill-team-calvin-gibbs-convicted (accessed February 9, 2013).

In Major Problems in the History of the Vietnam War, by Robert J. McMahon, 159-65. Lexington: D.C. Heath and Company, 1995.

McNamara, Robert S. *In Retrospect, The Tragedy and Lessons of Vietnam*. New York: Time Books, 1995.

Moore, Hal, and Colonel Hieu. LZ X-Ray After Action Report LTC Hal Moore and Colonel Hieu. September 01, 2008. http://www.generalhieu.com/lzxray_moore_hieu-2.htm (accessed December 11, 2012).

Mueller, John E. *War, President and Public Opinion*. New York: John Wiley & Sons, Inc, 1973.

Naveh, Shimon. *In Pursuit of Military Excellence, The Evolution of Operational Theory*. Portland, OR: Frank Cass, 1997.

Nixon, Richard Milhous. *A New Road for America*. Garden City: Doubleday, 1972.

—. *The Memoirs of Richard Nixon*. New York: Warner Books, 1978.

—. *The Real War*. New York: Warner Books, 1980.

Nye, Joseph S. and Welch, David A. *Understanding Global Conflict and Cooperation: An Introduction to Theory and History*. New York: Pearson Education, Inc., 2011.

Nye, Joseph S., Jr. "American Strategy after Bipolarity." *International Affairs* 66 (1990): 513-521.

—. *The Paradox of American Power*. Oxford: Oxford University Press, 2002.

O' Sullivan, Christopher. *Colin Powell: American Power and Intervention from Vietnam to Iraq*. Maryland: Rowman & Littlefield Publishers, 2009.

Obama, Barack H. "Remarks by the President in Address to the Nation on the Way Forward in Afghanistan and Pakistan." www.whitehouse.gov. December 1, 2009. http://www.whitehouse.gov/the-press-office/remarks-president-address-nation-way-forward-afghanistan-and-pakistan (accessed April 3, 2013).

Peters, Gerhard, and John T Woolley. Richard Nixon: Address to the Nation on the Situation in Southeast Asia. April 30, 1970. http://www.presidency.ucsb.edu/ws/index.php?pid=2490# (accessed March 5, 2013).

Pfeffer, Richard M. *No More Vietnams? The War and the Future of American Foregin Policy*. New York: Harper & Row, Publishers.

Ricks, Thomas E. *The Gamble: General David Petraeus and the American Military Adventure in Iraq, 2006-2008*. New York: The Penguin Press, 2009.

Robbins, James S. National Review. January 18, 2002. http://old.nationalreview.com/contributors/robbins011802.shtml (accessed March 10, 2013).

Robinson, Linda. *Tell Me How This Ends: General David Petraeus and the Search for a Way Out of Iraq*. New York: PublicAffairs, 2008.

Shaw, John M. *The Cambodian Campaign: the 1970 Offensive and America's Vietnam War*. Lawrence: University Press of Kansas, 2005.

Sheehan, Neil. *The Pentagon Papers: As Published by the New York Times* . Toronto, New York: Bantam Books , 1971.

Sheehan, Neil, Fox Butterfield, Hendrick Smith, and E. W. Kenworthy. *The Pentagon Papers: The Secret History of the Vietnam War*. New York: Quadrangle Books, 1971.

Snider, Don M., and Suzanne C. Nielsen. *American Civil-Military Relations: The Soldier and the State in a New Era*. Baltimore: The Johns Hopkins University Press, 2009.

Sorley, Lewis. *Thunderbolt, General Creighton Abrams and the Army of His Time*. Bloomington: Indiana University Press, 2008.

Sun-Tzu. *The Art of Warfare*. Edited by Robert G. Henricks. Translated by Roger T. Ames. New York: Ballantine Books, 1993.

Taylor, Maxwell D. *Swords and Plowshares*. New York: W.W Norton & Company, 1972.

The BDM Corporation. *The Strategic Lessons Learned in Vietnam Omibus Executive Summary*. McLean: Department of the Army, 1980.

The Pentagon Papers; the Defense Department History of United States Decisionmaking on Vietnam . The Senator Gravel ed. Boston: Beacon Press, 1971.

Thucydides. *The Landmark Thucydides: A Comprehensive Guide to the Peloponnesian War*. New York: Free Press, 1998.

True, J. L., B. D. Jones, and F. R. Baumgartner. "Punctuated-Equilibrium Theory." In *Theories of the Policy Process*, by Paul A Sabatier, edited by Paul A Sabatier, 155-88. Boulder: Westview Press, 2007.

Westmoreland, William C. *A Soldier Reports*. New York: Da Capo Press, Inc., 1989.

Willbanks, James H. *Abandoning Vietnam, How America Left and South Vietnam Lost Its War*. Lawrence, KS: University Press of Kansas, 2008.

Wilson, Colonel Gregory. "Anatomy of a Successful COIN Operation: OEF-Philippines and the Indirect Approach." *Military Review*, November-December 2006: 2-12.

Zielbauer, Paul von. "Army Says Improper Orders by Colonel Led to 4 Deaths." nytimes.com. Janurary 21, 2007. http://www.nytimes.com/2007/01/21/world/middleeast/21abuse.html?_r=1& (accessed February 9, 2013).

www.ingramcontent.com/pod-product-compliance
Lightning Source LLC
Chambersburg PA
CBHW080548290526
45790CB00006B/2592